Defy Roman Catholicism

An easy-to-read and concise rebuttal of
Roman Catholicism

Sonny L. Hernandez

"**I defy the Pope and all his laws**; and if God spare my life, ere many years, I will cause a boy that driveth the plow shall know more of the Scripture than thou dost."

~ William Tyndale

χάρις ὑμῖν καὶ εἰρήνη ἀπὸ Θεοῦ πατρὸς ἡμῶν
καὶ Κυρίου Ἰησοῦ Χριστοῦ.

For His Glory!

Table of Contents

PREFACE

I was raised in a nominal Roman Catholic home. As a young child, I remember seeing some family members pray to dead saints, make the sign of the cross when they ate, or they had statues or candles of Mary, along with paintings of Jesus in their homes.

My family trusted in baptism and works of supererogation as a means of salvation, which means they trusted in themselves, not the Savior. They loved relics, iconography and statues, not the imputed righteousness of the Savior. They trusted in their godless priests, not the pure gospel, and they held the pope in high esteem, which revealed that they worshiped and served Catholicism, not Christ.

However, I did not ever remember hearing a family member talk about the Bible, or have discussions about the good news of salvation. That is because my family, like most Roman Catholics, did not read the Bible, and thus did not know the true gospel.

During my childhood, I vividly recall when a few family members informed me that I was not saved because I had not been baptized. Albeit I challenged my family about Roman Catholic dogma, it was of no avail. All of my family members were raised Catholic, and many said, "We hold to Roman Catholic doctrine because we are Mexican, and that's what Mexicans believe."[1]

---

[1] This basically means that my family members held to Roman Catholicism because they loved tradition, not truth.

But God delivered me out of Roman Catholicism, and gave me Christ's righteousness.[2] The true gospel opened my eyes to trust in Christ's finished work, not my fallible will, which is why I vehemently believe salvation is by grace alone through faith alone in Christ alone. The true gospel also opened my eyes to see that Roman Catholics believe in doctrines of demons, and are led by a wolf in pope's clothing, so to speak.

Ever since God's Word revealed to me that Christ alone is the ground and assurance of my salvation, I have a strong desire to see my family members saved as Paul did for Israel.[3] I love my family members very much, and I do not look down on them, so to speak, because if it were not for the grace of God, I would still be lost.

Many families have suffered from unbiblical traditions, which appealed to race, not God's grace. This is why Christians need to evangelize Catholics with the true gospel.

[2] I knew when I was saved because God revealed His gospel to me in His word. Thus, I stopped looking to my self-righteousness, and I believed in the Savior's righteousness (Christ alone). As a disclaimer, Christians should never assume one is saved simply because they say they are; nor should Christians presumptuously or imprudently call someone a "brother" or "sister" in Christ. The only way to know if one is saved or has assurance is by judging the gospel that one professes to believe.

[3] See Romans 10:1-3: "Brethren, my heart's desire and prayer to God for Israel is, that they might be saved. For I bear them record that they have a zeal of God, but not according to knowledge. For they being ignorant of God's righteousness, and going about to establish their own righteousness, have not submitted themselves unto the righteousness of God."

Nonetheless, many Catholics will hate the truth contained in this book.[4] Many so-called Christians will also be offended by the content in this book that seeks to evangelize Catholics, but they do not witness to Catholics at all. However, it's hypocritical of one's so-called Christianity to be offended that born-again believers would evangelize lost Catholics, but are not offended that God is slandered by Roman Catholics.

In *Defy Roman Catholicism*, I have written an easy-to-read analysis and concise rebuttal of Roman Catholicism, which are lectures I wrote as part of a sermon series at Trinity Gospel Church in Shelbyville, KY. As a disclaimer, this book is not an exhaustive study of Roman Catholicism, but is simply a concise analysis and rebuttal of a few popish doctrines.

My prayer is that this book will point several of my family members to God's Word, and the truth contained therein will reveal to them that salvation is grounded in Christ's righteousness, not Roman Catholicism. I also pray that God's elect can use this book as a resource to evangelize Catholics with love. May God's will be done. For His Glory!

Sonny Hernandez
Trinity Gospel Church, KY

---

[4] John 15:18-19 states, "If the world hate you, ye know that it hated me before it hated you. If ye were of the world, the world would love his own: but because ye are not of the world, but I have chosen you out of the world, therefore the world hateth you."

CHAPTER 1

INTRODUCTION:
DEFY ROMAN CATHOLIC DOGMA

The Roman Catholic denomination is a very large religion and it is embraced by an alarming amount of people throughout the world. Nonetheless, there are several reasons why the Roman Catholic denomination and their doctrines should be excoriated, not embraced.[5]

Roman Catholicism denies *Sola Scriptura*,[6] which means the views of the Catholic tradition are blasphemous, not biblical. But the Bible teaches that God's Word or *Sola Scriptura* is the only sufficient, inerrant, and infallible rule of faith.[7]

---

[5] In this book, I will cite from the Catechisms of the Catholic Church (CCC). *Catechism of the Catholic Church.* (n.d.). Retrieved July 5, 2022, from https://www.vatican.va/archive/ENG0015/_INDEX.HTM. All references from this aforementioned source will be cited in the following manner: for example, CCC 2068.

[6] CCC 82: "As a result the Church, to whom the transmission and interpretation of Revelation is entrusted, "does not derive her certainty about all revealed truths from the holy Scriptures alone. **Both Scripture and Tradition must be accepted and honoured with equal sentiments of devotion and reverence**" (emphasis mine). Also see CCC 97, which states, "**Sacred Tradition *and* Sacred Scripture** make up a single sacred deposit of the Word of God..." (emphasis mine).

[7] Proverbs 30:5-6 states, "Every word of God is pure: he is a shield unto them that put their trust in him. Add thou not unto his words, lest he reprove thee, and thou be found a liar." Also see 2 Timothy 3:16-17. This passage states, "All scripture is given by inspiration of God, and is profitable for doctrine, for

Roman Catholicism does not teach *Sola Gratia* because it appeals to a false gospel,[8] not God's free grace. But the Bible teaches that only God has free will, not man,[9] and the source of justification is God's free and particular grace.[10]

Roman Catholicism maintains that one's superstitious free will is more superior than the Savior's finished work.[11] But the Bible teaches that the merits of Christ or the imputed righteousness of the Savior is the only ground and assurance of

---

reproof, for correction, for instruction in righteousness: That the man of God may be perfect, thoroughly furnished unto all good works."

[8] CCC 2068 states, "…so that all men may attain salvation through faith, Baptism and the observance of the Commandments." But the Bible says, "For by grace are ye saved through faith; and that **not of yourselves**: it is the gift of God: **Not of works**, lest any man should boast" (Ephesians 2:8-9). Thus, Roman Catholics do not receive and rest upon Christ's righteousness alone because they believe the law and their fallible works can save instead of the Savior's finished work alone.

[9] For example, Romans 3:24 says, "Being justified **freely** by his grace through the redemption that is in Christ Jesus" (emphasis mine), but the Bible never says man freely chooses God. Thus, people who think they have free will to accept God are delusional sinners, not delivered saints.

[10] The Bible does not teach universal, prevenient, or common grace. When the context of Scripture explicitly refers to *God's grace*, it is always particular, free, immutable, efficacious, irresistible, and exclusively reserved for the elect, not reprobate.

[11] CCC 1731: "Freedom is the power, rooted in reason and will, to act or not to act, to do this or that, and so to perform deliberate actions on one's own responsibility. **By free will one shapes one's own life. Human freedom is a force for growth and maturity in truth and goodness; it attains its perfection when directed toward God**, our beatitude" (emphasis mine).

salvation. Thus, true Christians won't look to the heresy of Rome,[12] but to His righteousness, which is perfect, not putative!

Roman Catholicism promotes dead works (CCC 2068), not the work of Christ (2 Corinthians 5:21). But the Bible teaches that works have never saved one soul from hell (Romans 3:28; Galatians 5:4; Ephesians 2:8-9), which is why true saints or believers embrace the meritorious work of Christ alone, without reservation.

Roman Catholicism teaches that salvation is conditioned on the sinner,[13] not the Savior. But the Bible teaches that Christ alone satisfied the demands of the divine law, and Christ alone died a substitutionary and propitiatory death on behalf of the elect, which refers to the whole work of Christ's righteousness in its compact unity (Romans 3:22, 24-25; 4:5-8; 5:17-19; Titus 3:5).

---

[12] Instead of believing in the biblical doctrine of imputed righteousness, Roman Catholics believe in infused righteousness, which puts the emphasis on cooperation and works, not the work of Christ alone. Asserting that one's cooperation with God is absolutely necessary to merit the righteousness that is required for salvation is popery, known as infused righteousness, or synergism. This type of papist rhetoric is not faithful or godly; it's a false gospel.

[13] CCC 1821: "We can therefore hope in the glory of heaven promised by God to those who love him and do his will. In every circumstance, each one of us should hope, with the grace of God, to persevere "to the end" and to obtain the joy of heaven, **as God's eternal reward for the good works accomplished with the grace of Christ**..." (emphasis mine).

Roman Catholicism endorses baptismal regeneration.[14] But the Bible never teaches that water can transform a child of wrath into a child of God; nor does the Bible say that water can regenerate a dead sinner into a delivered saint, which means Roman Catholicism elevates baptismal ceremonies above the blood of Christ. Thus, only the blood of Christ washes a believer's soul.[15]

Roman Catholicism rejects *Sola Fide*,[16] which indicates that this denomination is godless and corrupt, not gospel centered. But the Bible teaches that faith is a gift of God (Acts 10:44; 13:38-39; Galatians 2:16; Ephesians 2:7-9; Philippians 3:9), a

---

[14] CCC 1257: "**The Lord himself affirms that Baptism is necessary for salvation**. He also commands his disciples to proclaim the Gospel to all nations and to baptize them. Baptism is necessary for salvation for those to whom the Gospel has been proclaimed and who have had the possibility of asking for this sacrament. The Church does not know of any means other than Baptism that assures entry into eternal beatitude; this is why she takes care not to neglect the mission she has received from the Lord to see that all who can be baptized are "reborn of water and the Spirit." **God has bound salvation to the sacrament of Baptism**, but he himself is not bound by his sacraments" (emphasis mine).

[15] See 1 Peter 1:18-19: "Forasmuch as ye know that ye were not redeemed with corruptible things, AS silver and gold, from your vain conversation received by tradition from your fathers; **But with the precious blood of Christ**, as of a lamb without blemish and without spot" (emphasis mine).

[16] Catholics conflate faith and works, and many of them believe their faith saved them, or they think their faith precedes regeneration, or they will argue that faith is not a gift of God. But faith is not the cause or ground of justification, and faith does not precede regeneration. Faith is a gift and work of God. Also, see Hebrews 11:1, "Now faith is the substance of things hoped for, the evidence of things not seen."

work of God, and the means or alone instrument of justification, whereby God's particular people are justified by faith alone because of the merits of Christ alone (Romans 3:28; 5:1).

Roman Catholicism elevates men's decisions above the Master's decree (CCC 1743-1747). But the Bible unequivocally teaches that God determined or decreed all things (Isaiah 46:10; Ephesians 1:11), and it undeniably maintains that salvation is of the Lord (Jonah 2:9), not man.

Roman Catholicism refers to the pope with a title that is only given to God the Father,[17] which means calling the pope "Holy Father" is not Scriptural, but Satanic. But the Bible teaches that Holy Father refers to the first person of the Trinity,[18] not a false prophet [pope] who loves traditions.

Roman Catholicism gives the pope a title that is only ascribed to Christ, which indicates that the pope is a child of hell, not the head of the church.[19] But the Bible teaches that *head of the church* is

---

[17] Richard Bennett and Mike Gendron are two notable apologists to Roman Catholics who have written extensively and published several videos on the pope referring to himself with names or roles that are given to the Triune God.

[18] 1 Corinthians 8:6 states, "But to us there is but one God, the Father, of whom are all things, and we in him; and one Lord Jesus Christ, by whom are all things, and we by him."

[19] CCC 883: "The college or body of bishops has no authority unless united with the **Roman Pontiff, Peter's successor, as its head**." As such, this college has "supreme and full authority over the universal Church; but this power cannot be exercised without the agreement of the Roman Pontiff" (emphasis mine).

reserved exclusively for the sinless Master (Ephesians 1:22; 5:23; Colossians 1:18), not a sinful man.

Roman Catholicism calls the pope "vicar of Christ,"[20] which refers to the Holy Spirit (John 14:16), revealing the pope is truly anti-Christ, not God's representative on earth. But God's Word teaches that referring to sinful men with roles that belong to God alone is prohibited, not permitted.

Roman Catholicism teaches unbiblical views about Mary by ardently maintaining that she was the mother of God (CCC 495) who was born sinless (CCC 490-493), remained a virgin (CCC 499), was taken up body and soul to heaven (CCC 966), and is co-redemptrix or mediatrix (CCC 969). But the Bible teaches that Mary was a sinner,[21] and she did not remain a virgin (Matthew 13:55-56). Additionally, the Bible does not say that Mary ascended bodily into heaven, and God's Word teaches that the only mediator between God and man is Christ (1 Timothy 2:5). Thus, holding to Mariology is rank heresy, not a holy ritual.

---

[20] CCC 882: "The Pope, Bishop of Rome and Peter's successor, "is the perpetual and visible source and foundation of the unity both of the bishops and of the whole company of the faithful." "For the Roman Pontiff, by reason of his **office as Vicar of Christ**, and as pastor of the entire Church has full, supreme, and universal power over the whole Church, a power which he can always exercise unhindered"" (emphasis mine).

[21] Mary acknowledged that she was a sinner because she said, "And my spirit hath rejoiced in God my **Saviour**" (Luke 1:47, emphasis mine).

Roman Catholicism teaches transubstantiation, which basically promotes cannibalism, and it maintains that the body of the Savior is ubiquitous.[22] Additionally, the unbiblical Roman Catholic Mass denies the completed and saving work of Christ. But the Bible teaches that Christ died a substitutionary and propitiatory death for the elect (with respect to His humanity), and the Savior said, "It is finished" (John 19:30), which is in the perfect tense, indicating that Christ's sacrifice does not ever need to take place again.[23]

Roman Catholicism promotes graven images,[24] which proves this denomination is evil, not ethical. But the Word of God teaches that graven

---

[22] CCC 1376: "The Council of Trent summarizes the Catholic faith by declaring: "Because Christ our Redeemer said that it was truly his body that he was offering under the species of bread, it has always been the conviction of the Church of God, and this holy Council now declares again, that by the consecration of the bread and wine there takes place a change of the whole substance of the bread into the substance of the body of Christ our Lord and of the whole substance of the wine into the substance of his blood. This change the holy Catholic Church has fittingly and properly called transubstantiation."' For more information on the doctrine of transubstantiation, see Dalcour, E. (2020, March 4). *Roman Catholicism and the Eucharist*. Department of Christian Defense. Retrieved July 8, 2022, from https://christiandefense.org/roman-catholicism/roman-catholicism-and-transubstantiation/

[23] Also, Christ resurrected for the justification of the elect, with respect to His divinity. Therefore, the Roman Catholic view of transubstantiation is doctrine from hell, not heaven.

[24] CCC 2141: "The veneration of sacred images is based on the mystery of the Incarnation of the Word of God. **It is not contrary to the first commandment**" (emphasis mine).

images are prohibited (Exodus 20:4-6; Isaiah 42:8), not permitted, because the one true God who is Tri-personal does not share glory with anyone.

Roman Catholicism does not teach that men and women should only pray to the sinless Savior, but also to dead saints and sinners (CCC 1014, 2679, 2683). But the Word of God teaches that prayers are to be made to the Triune God (Philippians 4:6), not to dead sinners that cannot hear them.

Therefore, Roman Catholicism appeals to Satan, not Scripture. So when a person says, "I am a devout Catholic," true Christians need to share these aforementioned truths above with them, and say, "If you embrace Roman Catholicism, then you reject Christ's righteousness" (Galatians 1:8).

The only cure for Roman Catholics is the gospel, which is grounded in the Trinity, and thus points to the Father's unconditional election, the Son's particular and saving death, and the Spirit's sealing of those whom the Father gave to Christ. May God's will be done. Amen.

STUDY QUESTIONS

1. If you were raised Roman Catholic, what were some of the reasons your family held to Roman Catholic doctrine?

2. Why is Romans 10:1-3 important when evangelizing to Roman Catholics?

3. Does Roman Catholicism deny *Sola Scriptura*?

4. Contrast CCC 82 with 2 Timothy 3:16-17 and explain what the differences are.

5. Read CCC 2068 and also Ephesians 2:8-9 and explain in your own words why Roman Catholicism is not biblical.

6. What is the only ground and assurance of salvation?

7. Explain the Roman Catholic doctrine of infused righteousness.

8. Which biblical text teaches that works do not save?

9. Does Roman Catholicism endorse baptismal regeneration?

10. How do Roman Catholics reject *Sola Fide*?

11. Does the Bible teach that faith is a gift from God?

12. Is it biblical to call the pope "Holy Father?"

13. The head of the church is reserved exclusively for whom?

14. Why is it wrong to call the pope "vicar of Christ?"

15. Was Mary born sinless?

16. Do Catholics believe Mary was taken up body and soul to heaven?

17. Explain in your own words why Mariology is rank heresy.

18. What does the Roman Catholic doctrine of transubstantiation promote?

19. Read CCC 1376 and explain why it is heretical.

20. What does the Roman Catholic Mass deny?

21. Does Roman Catholicism promote graven images?

22. Are graven images prohibited in Scripture?

23. Should prayers be made to dead sinners?

24. What would you say to someone who professes to be a "devout Catholic"?

25. What is the only cure for Roman Catholics?

CHAPTER 2

DEFY THE POPE: ANTI-CHRIST, NOT AUTHENTIC CHRISTIAN

The pope is known to many as the bishop of Rome, or the Roman pontiff, etc. This so-called leader of the Roman Catholic denomination is also insolently and imprudently referred to as Peter's successor, Holy Father, head of the church, and the vicar of Christ by Catholics worldwide. This means a lot of people are deceived, not delivered.[25]

Many so-called devout Catholics are enamored by popish doctrines, which is why they love Catholic dogma, but loathe Christian doctrine.

------

[25] The Bible teaches that some men don't believe the truth because they are spiritually discerned. First Corinthians 2:14 states, "But the natural man receiveth not the things of the Spirit of God: for they are foolishness unto him: neither can he know them, because they are spiritually discerned." Moreover, Romans 1:28 teaches that God actively reprobated the wicked. This passage states, "And even as they did not like to retain God in their knowledge, God gave them over to a reprobate mind, to do those things which are not convenient." Furthermore, John 12:39-40 teaches that God actively blinded the eyes and hardened the hearts of the wicked so they could not believe. "Therefore they could not believe, because that Esaias said again, He hath blinded their eyes, and hardened their heart; that they should not see with their eyes, nor understand with their heart, and be converted, and I should heal them." But the Bible also teaches that God knows who are His. See 2 Timothy 2:19, which states, "Nevertheless the foundation of God standeth sure, having this seal, The Lord knoweth them that are his. And, Let every one that nameth the name of Christ depart from iniquity."

As a result, Catholics will yield and obey a sinful pope, not the purity of Scripture.[26]

Although Catholics are duped by the pope, Bible believers are not. God's people are aware that the pope is anti-Christ, not an authentic Christian. Additionally, the saints know the pope is not holy or faithful, but is a heretic and a false teacher.[27]

Christians know the pope is a child of hell, not the head of the church, because they appeal to Scripture alone, and thus judge all professions of faith with the true gospel. All Christians need to do is examine Catholic doctrine, and read the Bible, to see that Catholicism is not Christian.

Therefore, the purpose of this chapter is not to provide an exhaustive analysis and disputation on the papacy, but to simply demonstrate, in three basic points, that the Roman Catholic pope is anti-Christ because his role or so-called office attempts to rob the Triune God of glory.

---

[26] Christians need to lovingly preach the gospel to Catholics, and tell them, "There is a way which seemeth right unto a man, but the end thereof are the ways of death" (Proverbs 14:12).

[27] A heretic man is one who denies the authority of Scripture alone, promotes doctrines that are contrary to the true gospel, craves foolish disputes, and loves to lead people away from the truth. Titus 3:10-11 states, "A man that is an heretick after the first and second admonition reject; Knowing that he that is such is subverted, and sinneth, being condemned of himself."

Put another way, the CCC promotes papal infallibility, the CCC teaches that the pope is Peter's successor, and the CCC refers to the pope with names or roles that are ascribed to the Triune God. But the Bible does not support the doctrines contained in the CCC, and the following points will explain why.

I. Roman Catholicism promotes papal infallibility, but the Bible teaches that the pope is a purveyor of iniquity.

Catholics believe in papal infallibility, which indicates that they think the pope is without error. But the Bible teaches that only God is infallible. Therefore, the doctrine of papal infallibility is heresy because it distorts the plain reading of Scripture, and it seeks to give adulation to a mere sinner [pope] in lieu of exalting God alone.

According to Catholic tradition, not Scripture, Christ endowed the so-called teaching office of the Catholic church with infallibility in matters of faith, which the pope enjoys.

CCC 890: The mission of the Magisterium is linked to the definitive nature of the covenant established by God with his people in Christ. It is this Magisterium's task to preserve God's people from deviations and defections and to guarantee them the objective possibility of professing the true faith without error. Thus, the pastoral duty of the Magisterium is aimed at seeing to it that the People of God abides in the truth that liberates. To fulfill this service, **Christ endowed the Church's shepherds**

with the charism of infallibility in matters of faith and morals. the exercise of this charism takes several forms:

CCC 891: "**The Roman Pontiff, head of the college of bishops, enjoys this infallibility in virtue of his office**, when, as supreme pastor and teacher of all the faithful - who confirms his brethren in the faith he proclaims by a definitive act a doctrine pertaining to faith or morals.... the infallibility promised to the Church is also present in the body of bishops when, together with Peter's successor, they exercise the supreme Magisterium," above all in an Ecumenical Council. **When the Church through its supreme Magisterium proposes a doctrine "for belief as being divinely revealed," and as the teaching of Christ, the definitions "must be adhered to with the obedience of faith." This infallibility extends as far as the deposit of divine Revelation itself**. (emphasis mine)

CCC 892: Divine assistance is also given to the successors of the apostles, teaching in communion with the successor of Peter, and, in a particular way, to the bishop of Rome, pastor of the whole Church, when, without arriving at an infallible definition and without pronouncing in a "definitive manner," they propose in the exercise of the ordinary Magisterium a teaching that leads to better understanding of Revelation in matters of faith and morals. To this ordinary teaching the faithful "are to adhere to it with religious assent" which, though distinct from the assent of faith, is nonetheless an extension of it.

The catechisms above appeal to self-righteousness, not the Savior's righteousness. God alone has infallibility, not man, but the Roman Catholic traditions seek to elevate a sinful man, not the sinless Master.[28]

Even the apostle Paul, Christ's chosen servant, never said in Scripture that he exercised infallibility in matters of faith and morals that he enjoyed.[29] Paul rejoiced in Christ,[30] while the pope revels in Catholicism.

---

[28] When men say "I am," in any context, it's insignificant because all men are fallible, and sinful creatures who derive from dust. But when Christ said "I AM" (John 8:58), it is significant and compelling because it points to His eternality, immutability, impeccability, and consubstantiality. As the great "I AM," the all-sufficient and preexistent Savior is true God from true God, the ultimate agent of creation, and the apocalyptic judge of all humanity.

[29] Read Roman 7, and see that Paul never argued that he was infallible, but said, "… I am carnal, sold under sin" (v. 14), "…what I hate, that do I" (v. 15), "…sin that dwelleth in me" (v. 17), "For I know that in me (that is, in my flesh,) dwelleth no good thing…" (v. 18), "… evil is present with me" (v. 21), and "O wretched man that I am! who shall deliver me from the body of this death" (v. 24)?

[30] See Philippians 3:8-9. This passage states, "Yea doubtless, and I count all things but loss for the excellency of the knowledge of Christ Jesus my Lord: for whom I have suffered the loss of all things, and do count them but dung, that I may win Christ, And be found in him, not having mine own righteousness, which is of the law, but that which is through the faith of Christ, the righteousness which is of God by faith."

The apostle Paul boasted in the Savior,[31] not himself, whereas the pope boasts in his Catholicism, not Christ. Paul never boasted in himself because he was a fallible and sinful creature who trusted in Holy Scripture, not human tradition.

Moreover, claiming to have infallibility is nothing more than self-aggrandizement for the pope, a fallible man, to draw his acolytes away from the fact that only God is infallible. According to Scripture, only God is perfect, only God does not change, only God is infallible, and only God is righteous:

God is perfect

> **2 Samuel 22:31**: "As for God, his way is perfect; the word of the LORD is tried: he is a buckler to all them that trust in him."

> **Matthew 5:48**: "Be ye therefore perfect, even as your Father which is in heaven is perfect."

God does not change

> **Malachi 3:6**: "For I am the LORD, I change not; therefore ye sons of Jacob are not consumed."

> **Hebrews 13:8**: "Jesus Christ the same yesterday, and to day, and for ever."

---

[31] In Galatians 6:14, Paul said, "But God forbid that I should glory, save in the cross of our Lord Jesus Christ, by whom the world is crucified unto me, and I unto the world."

God does not fail

> **Joshua 21:45**: "There failed not ought of any good thing which the LORD had spoken unto the house of Israel; all came to pass."

> **Isaiah 46:10**: "Declaring the end from the beginning, and from ancient times the things that are not yet done, saying, My counsel shall stand, and I will do all my pleasure."

God is righteous

> **Psalm 119:137**: "Righteous art thou, O LORD, and upright are thy judgments."

The Bible is also patently clear that the doctrine of papal infallibility is not heterodoxy; it is heresy. This is due to the fact that Scripture, God's infallible Word, teaches that all men are fallible sinners.[32]

All men are sinners by nature

---

[32] According to Turretin, "Man cannot be the infallible interpreter of the Scriptures and judge of controversies because he is liable to error. Our faith cannot be placed in him, but upon God alone from whom depends the sense and meaning of the Scriptures and who is the best interpreter of his own words. As the only teacher, he can best explain the meaning of the law (Mt. 23:8, 10); our lawgiver who is able to save and to destroy (Jam. 4:12)..." Francis Turretin, *Institutes of Elenctic Theology* (G. M. Giger, Trans., J. T. Dennison, Ed.). Vol. 2 (Phillipsburg, PA: P&R Publishing, 1992), 156. All subsequent references will be cited as: Turretin, 2:633.

Romans 3:23: "For all have sinned, and come short of the glory of God."

Romans 5:12: "Wherefore, as by one man sin entered into the world, and death by sin; and so death passed upon all men, for that all have sinned."

All men are conceived in sin

Psalm 51:5: "Behold, I was shapen in iniquity; and in sin did my mother conceive me."

All men are born as children of wrath

Ephesians 2:3: "Among whom also we all had our conversation in times past in the lusts of our flesh, fulfilling the desires of the flesh and of the mind; and were by nature the children of wrath, even as others."

All men are desperately wicked as can be

Genesis 6:5: "And GOD saw that the wickedness of man was great in the earth, and that every imagination of the thoughts of his heart was only evil continually."

All men are unrighteous

Isaiah 64:6: "But we are all as an unclean thing, and all our righteousnesses are as filthy rags; and we all do fade as a leaf; and our iniquities, like the wind, have taken us away."

Therefore, only God is infallible and sovereign, whereas all men are fallible sinners, which means the doctrine of papal infallibility must be rejected. The leader of the Catholic tradition is an iniquitous papist, not Peter's successor, which will now be addressed.

II. Roman Catholicism teaches that the pope is Peter's successor, but the Bible teaches that he is a sinful papist.

Another popular belief among Roman Catholics is the delirious view that the pastoral office of Peter was assigned to Catholic leaders under the primacy of the pope. So Catholics believe the pope is not only infallible, but they also believe he is literally Peter's successor, which can be seen below:

> CCC 880: When Christ instituted the Twelve, "he constituted [them] in the form of a college or permanent assembly, at the head of which he placed Peter, chosen from among them." Just as "by the Lord's institution, St. Peter and the rest of the apostles constitute a single apostolic college, **so in like fashion the Roman Pontiff, Peter's successor**, and the bishops, the successors of the apostles, are related with and united to one another."

> CCC 881: **The Lord made Simon alone, whom he named Peter, the "rock" of his Church**. He gave him the keys of his Church and instituted him shepherd of the whole flock. "The office of binding and loosing which was given to Peter was also assigned to

the college of apostles united to its head." This pastoral office of Peter and the other apostles belongs to the Church's very foundation and is continued by the bishops under the primacy of the Pope.

CCC 882: **The Pope**, **Bishop of Rome and Peter's successor**, "is the perpetual and visible source and foundation of the unity both of the bishops and of the whole company of the faithful." "For the Roman Pontiff, by reason of his office as Vicar of Christ, and as pastor of the entire Church has full, supreme, and universal power over the whole Church, a power which he can always exercise unhindered."

CCC 883: "The college or body of bishops has no authority unless united with the Roman Pontiff, **Peter's successor**, **as its head**." As such, this college has "supreme and full authority over the universal Church; but this power cannot be exercised without the agreement of the Roman Pontiff."

CCC 884: "The college of bishops exercises power over the universal Church in a solemn manner in an ecumenical council." But "**there never is an ecumenical council which is not confirmed or at least recognized as such by Peter's successor**." (emphasis mine)

As noted above, Roman Catholicism teaches that Peter is the rock of the church, but Ephesians 2:20 states, "And are built upon the foundation of the apostles and prophets, **Jesus Christ himself being the chief corner stone**" (emphasis mine).

Thus, Roman Catholics believe the pope is Peter's successor because they are ignoring the context of Matthew 16:13-20, and their godless priests have twisted this text so they can elevate the Catholic pope above Peter's confession. Examine the context:

> **Matthew 16:13-20**: "[13]When Jesus came into the coasts of Caesarea Philippi, he asked his disciples, saying, Whom do men say that I the Son of man am? [14]And they said, Some say that thou art John the Baptist: some, Elias; and others, Jeremias, or one of the prophets. [15]He saith unto them, But whom say ye that I am? [16]And Simon Peter answered and said, Thou art the Christ, the Son of the living God. [17]And Jesus answered and said unto him, Blessed art thou, Simon Barjona: for flesh and blood hath not revealed it unto thee, but my Father which is in heaven. [18]And I say also unto thee, That thou art Peter, and upon this rock I will build my church; and the gates of hell shall not prevail against it. [19]And I will give unto thee the keys of the kingdom of heaven: and whatsoever thou shalt bind on earth shall be bound in heaven: and whatsoever thou shalt loose on earth shall be loosed in heaven. [20]Then charged he his disciples that they should tell no man that he was Jesus the Christ."

In the excerpt above, Christ never said, "Whom do men say that *you* are, Peter?" On the contrary, Christ provided the underlying theme of Matthew 16:13-20 when he said, "…Whom do men say that **I the Son of man am**" (emphasis mine)? Peter confessed Christ because God gave him the gift of faith to believe, which is why Christ said, "…Blessed art thou, Simon Barjona: for flesh and blood hath not revealed it unto thee, but my Father which is in heaven."[33]

After Peter confessed the Lord because of the merits of Christ, Jesus said, "And I say also unto thee, That thou art Peter, **and upon this rock I will build my church**; and the gates of hell shall not prevail against it" (Matthew 16:18, emphasis mine).

According to CCC 881, "The Lord made Simon alone, whom he named Peter, the "rock" of his Church…," but Christ never said, "Peter, you are the rock" in Matthew 16:18. When Christ said, "…upon this," it's important to note that *tautn* [Gk. "ταύτη"; "this"] is a demonstrative pronoun, which cannot be referring to *Petros* [Gk. "Πέτρος"; "Peter"] because ταύτη is feminine, whereas *Πέτρος* is masculine. Thus, the antecedent of *ταύτη* is referring to Peter's faith in Jesus,[34] the chief corner stone.

---

[33] Faith is a gift of God, which can be seen in 2 Peter 1:1. This passage states, "Simon Peter, a servant and an apostle of Jesus Christ, **to them that have obtained like precious faith with us through the righteousness of God and our Saviour Jesus Christ**" (emphasis mine).

[34] According to the Department of Christian Defense, "Demonstrative pronouns ("this, that") can express an indirect significance as with a third person pronoun, thus expressing a

Additionally, the Department of Christian Defense provided biblical and compelling arguments against the Roman Catholic view of the primacy of Peter.

> 1) There is no biblical evidence indicating that Peter had supremacy over all the other apostles.

> 2) Peter never once considered that he was Pope, Pontiff; Vicar of Christ, Holy Father, or Head of the whole Christian Church, nor did any of the other apostles make such as claim.

> 3) Peter outwardly denied the Lord (out of fear) and Peter was rebuked by the Apostle Paul for being prejudice against the Gentiles (cf. Gal. 2:11-12).

> 4) At the first church council in Jerusalem (not Rome), it was James and not Peter who was the leading speaker and decision maker, for James authoritatively declared Acts 15:19– "It is my judgment that we do not trouble those who are turning to God from among the Gentiles." Moreover, the letter that was sent out regarding the judgment never mentions Peter (cf. v. 23).

---

thing ("this") other than a direct reference." Dalcour, E. (2018, February 8). *Roman Catholicism's false (a-historical) view of Matthew 16:18 regarding the identification of the "Rock" as Peter*. Department of Christian Defense. Retrieved July 12, 2022, from https://christiandefense.org/roman-catholicism/catholicism-and-the-primacy-of-the-apostle-peter/#_ftn4. See note 3 at the bottom of page.

5) At the end of Romans, Paul sends his greetings to at least 26 people—but Peter is not even mentioned! Why? Surely, if Peter had "recognized supremacy" over Rome and all the apostles, we would expect Paul to have greeted him first!

6) Peter was a married man, unlike the Roman Popes (cf, Matt. 8:14; 1 Cor. 9:5).[35]

Thus far, this chapter has demonstrated that the Roman Catholic doctrine of papal infallibility, the primacy of Peter, and the view that Peter's successor is the pope are anti-Christian doctrines, unbiblical traditions, and radical heresies.

But these aforementioned doctrines are not the only heresies that are taught in the Roman Catholic tradition. There are many more. This chapter will now address how the pope refers to himself with names or roles that are given to the Triune God.[36]

III. Roman Catholicism ascribes names or roles to the pope that are given to the Triune God, which is blasphemous, not biblical.

---

[35] Ibid.

[36] As stated in the introduction, Richard Bennett and Mike Gendron are two apologists who have written extensively or published videos on the pope ascribing names and roles to himself that belong to God. I am not endorsing these two apologists, but I have read and watched several of their articles and videos on the pope, which is why I provided this disclaimer because I have learned a lot from some of their videos and articles.

a. "Holy Father"

Referring to the pope with names or roles that belong to the Triune God is despicable. According to Scripture, the pope, a mere man, is fallible, but the Father is superlatively holy. The pope is a sinner, but the Son is the Savior. And the pope is a created being, while the Spirit is the eternal helper.

Thus, *Holy Father* refers to God the Father, the *head of the church* points to the Son, and the *vicar of Christ* is the Holy Spirit, not the leader of the Roman Catholic denomination. But Roman Catholics will disagree since they love tradition, not the truth.

According to a former Roman Catholic priest, Richard Bennett, the Vatican calls the pope the "Holy Father," and they deny the gospel of Jesus Christ.

> A Christian's relationship with the Holy Father is crucial. Thus, Jesus Christ prayed, *"Holy Father, keep through thine own name those whom thou hast given me, that they may be one, as we are"* (John 17:11). Only those who have been placed in Christ Jesus by God's grace alone have the right and privilege to call Holy God their Father. Nevertheless, the Vatican both teaches a different gospel and, on its website, claims a successive chain of 266 "holy fathers," or popes, from St. Peter to Pope Francis.[37]

---

[37] Bennett, R. (n.d.). *Who is the True Holy Father: God or Pope Francis?* Berean Beacon. Retrieved July 13, 2022, from

Bennett rightfully explained that only the elect who were unconditionally chosen, and purchased by the particular and saving death of Christ, have the privilege of calling the Holy God their "Father."

But Roman Catholics call the pope, a sinful man, the "Holy Father," which cannot be supported in Scripture. Calling the pope "Holy Father" is blasphemy because the Bible teaches that the first person of the Trinity is the Holy Father.

> **Matthew 23:9**: "And call no man your father upon the earth: for one is your Father, which is in heaven."

> **1 Corinthians 8:6**: "But to us there is but one God, the Father, of whom are all things…"

> **Ephesians 1:3**: "Blessed be the God and Father of our Lord Jesus Christ, who hath blessed us with all spiritual blessings in heavenly places in Christ."

> **Ephesians 4:6**: "One God and Father of all, who is above all, and through all, and in you all."

b. "Head of Church"

Roman Catholics also call the pope, the so-called Roman pontiff, the "head of the church," but that title belongs only to Jesus Christ, God the Logos.

---

https://bereanbeacon.org/who-is-the-true-holy-father-god-or-pope-francis/

Yet Roman Catholics worldwide follow the teachings of their traditions, which cannot be supported with Scripture:

> CCC 879: Sacramental ministry in the Church, then, is a service exercised in the name of Christ. It has a personal character and a collegial form. This is evidenced by the bonds between the episcopal college **and its head, the successor of St. Peter**, and in the relationship between the bishop's pastoral responsibility for his particular church and the common solicitude of the episcopal college for the universal Church.

> CCC 881: The Lord made Simon alone, whom he named Peter, the "rock" of his Church. He gave him the keys of his Church and instituted him shepherd of the whole flock. "**The office of binding and loosing which was given to Peter was also assigned to the college of apostles united to its head**." This pastoral office of Peter and the other apostles belongs to the Church's very foundation and is continued by the bishops under the primacy of the Pope.

> CCC 883: "The college or body of bishops has no authority unless united with the Roman Pontiff, **Peter's successor, as its head**." As such, this college has "supreme and full authority over the universal Church; but this power cannot be exercised without the agreement of the Roman Pontiff."

CCC 899: The initiative of lay Christians is necessary especially when the matter involves discovering or inventing the means for permeating social, political, and economic realities with the demands of Christian doctrine and life. This initiative is a normal element of the life of the Church:

> Lay believers are in the front line of Church life; for them the Church is the animating principle of human society. Therefore, they in particular ought to have an ever-clearer consciousness not only of belonging to the Church, but of being the Church, that is to say, the community of the faithful on earth **under the leadership of the Pope, the common Head**, and of the bishops in communion with him. They are the Church.

CCC 936: The Lord made St. Peter the visible foundation of his Church. He entrusted the keys of the Church to him. **The bishop of the Church of Rome, successor to St. Peter, is "head of the college of bishops**, the Vicar of Christ and Pastor of the universal Church on earth" (CIC, can. 331). (emphasis mine)

As seen above, Roman Catholics believe the pope is the head of the church. But referring to the pope as the head of the church robs Christ of His glory, it usurps Christ's headship over the invisible church, and it denies the Lordship or full supremacy of Jesus Christ as king, savior, and judge.

According to Scripture, the inerrant, infallible, and sufficient Word of God, Christ is the head of the church, not the so-called Roman pontiff, which means the pope is a child of hell, not the head of the church. See the following Scriptures, which teach that Christ alone is the head of the church:

> **Ephesians 1:22**: "And hath put all things under his feet, and gave him to be the head over all things to the church."

> **Ephesians 5:23**: "For the husband is the head of the wife, even as Christ is the head of the church: and he is the saviour of the body."

> **Colossians 1:18**: "And he is the head of the body, the church: who is the beginning, the firstborn from the dead; that in all things he might have the preeminence."

> **Colossians 2:10**: "And ye are complete in him, which is the head of all principality and power."

Therefore, when Catholics say, "the pope is the head of the church," inform them that their arguments don't prove the point they are desperately trying to make; all their point proves is that they think a sinful pope is more superior than the purity of Scripture, which reveals that they are definitely Catholics, not delivered Christians.

c. "Vicar of Christ"

Roman Catholics not only refer to the pope with names or roles that belong to the Father and the Son, but they also call the pope the "vicar of Christ," which refers to the Holy Spirit. See the following evidence:

> CCC882: "The Pope, Bishop of Rome and Peter's successor," is the perpetual and visible source and foundation of the unity both of the bishops and of the whole company of the faithful." "For the Roman Pontiff, **by reason of his office as Vicar of Christ**, and as pastor of the entire Church has full, supreme, and universal power over the whole Church, a power which he can always exercise unhindered."

> CCC 936: The Lord made St. Peter the visible foundation of his Church. He entrusted the keys of the Church to him. The bishop of the Church of Rome, successor to St. Peter, is "head of the college of bishops, **the Vicar of Christ** and Pastor of the universal Church on earth" (CIC, can. 331). (emphasis mine)

Even though Roman Catholicism teaches that the pope is the vicar of Christ, it should be evident that there is no biblical justification for such a claim. This is due to the fact that God's Word does not teach that the pope, a sinful created being, would be Christ's representative who has "…full, supreme, and universal power over the whole Church, a power which he can always exercise unhindered" (CCC 882). Richard Bennett explained why this does not glorify Christ:

The counterfeit nature of the Pope's claim to be "the Vicar of Christ" is shown by his doctrine and deeds. The key role of the True Vicar of Christ is to glorify Christ, "He shall glorify me: for he shall receive of mine, and shall shew it unto you" (John 16:14). The sending of the Spirit was the glorifying of Christ. God the Father glorifies Christ Jesus in heaven, and the Spirit glorifies Him on earth. All the gifts and graces of the Holy Spirit are to glorify Christ. The Lord Jesus Christ promised the Apostles, "when he, the Spirit of truth, is come, he will guide you into all truth" (John 16:13). God's truth is an indissoluble, balanced and harmonious whole. In the Bible we have "all truth", in this the Holy Spirit truly glorifies Jesus Christ. In stark contrast, the Pope claims to possess "infallible teaching authority". This neither glorifies Christ nor honors the Spirit of truth. Also the Pope, as "the Vicar of Christ" teaches "rebirth" by baptism, which demeans the glory of Christ.

By crucifixes, rosaries, and scapulars, the earthly Vicar purports to fortify men and women against the assaults of Satan. He also maintains that indulgences can shorten the sufferings of souls in purgatory. While presiding over substantially the richest financial institution in the world, he maintains and advocates vows of poverty. Even as thousands of souls are corrupted by unbridled filthiness, he defends the vows of celibacy for his priests. By autonomous proclamations he releases men and women from their marriage vows in self- declared annulments. None of these deeds glorify Christ Jesus the Lord. The major enemy of Christ and His Gospel, however, is not materialism nor is it lust, but rather the spiritual pride and the apostasy of the very one who pretends to be His "Vicar". The first lie of Satan, "ye shall be as gods" (Genesis 3:5) reaches its full fruition in the Papal claim to be "Vicar of Christ". By this the words of the Apostle Paul are literally fulfilled, "who opposeth and exalteth himself above all that is called God…showing himself that he is God" (II Thessalonians 2:4).[38]

Bottom line: The vicar of Christ refers to the Holy Spirit. In John 14, Christ said, "…I will pray the Father, and he shall give you another Comforter, that he may abide with you for ever" (v. 16), and, "…the Comforter, which is the Holy Ghost, whom the Father will send in my name, he shall teach you all things, and bring all things to your remembrance, whatsoever I have said unto you" (v. 26). Therefore, the Roman Catholic view of the pope being the vicar of Christ is blasphemy.

IV. Closing

In closing, this chapter has shown that the pope is *not* infallible, the pope is *not* Peter's successor, the pope is *not* the Holy Father, the pope is *not* the head of the church, and the pope is *not* the

---

[38] Bennett, R. (n.d.). *Who is the True Vicar of Christ?* Berean Beacon. Retrieved July 13, 2022, from https://bereanbeacon.org/who-is-the-true-vicar-of-christ/

vicar of Christ. According to Scripture, the pope is a sinner, not a saint, and all of the Catholic catechism teachings on the pope are not from heaven, but hell.

STUDY QUESTIONS

1. Christians should judge all professions of faith with what?

2. A heretic man is one who does what?

3. What is the doctrine of papal infallibility?

4. Explain several reasons why papal infallibility is egregious heresy.

5. Does the Roman Catholic tradition teach that the pope is Peter's successor?

6. Roman Catholics believe the pope is Peter's successor because they are ignoring the context of what biblical passage?

7. What is the context of Matthew 16:18?

8. Explain some compelling arguments that refute the Roman Catholic view that Peter was a pope.

9. Roman Catholicism ascribes names or roles to the pope that are given to whom?

10. Explain some reasons why calling the pope "Holy Father" is not biblical.

11. Explain which Roman Catholic catechisms teach that the pope is the head of the church.

12. Explain several reasons why calling the pope "the head of the church" is blasphemous.

13. Which biblical text teaches that Christ is the head of the church?

14. How would you evangelize a Roman Catholic who believes the pope is the head of the church?

15. Explain a few times in your life that witnessing to Roman Catholics has been difficult.

16. Read CCC 882 and CCC 936 and explain what the pope is called that is unbiblical.

17. Does the Bible teach that the pope is the vicar of Christ?

18. Why did Richard Bennett argue that referring to the pope as the vicar of Christ does not glorify Jesus?

19. Which biblical text teaches that the Holy Spirit is the vicar of Christ?

20. After reading this chapter, explain in your own words how you feel that you are more equipped to witness to Roman Catholics.

21. What difficulties do you think you may encounter while evangelizing Roman Catholics?

22. According to Scripture, do you think the pope is anti-Christ?

23. If you have a family member that esteemed the pope, what would you say?

24. Explain in your own words how you would share the gospel to a Roman Catholic.

25. Do you pray for Roman Catholics to be saved?

CHAPTER 3

DEFY MARIOLOGY MYTHS

Historically, Roman Catholics are known for saying the "hail Mary" prayer, Roman Catholics will pray to Mary, Roman Catholics will give reverence to statues of Mary, and Roman Catholics will offer special devotion or worship to Mary, which is blasphemous and idolatrous, not biblical integrity.

In an attempt to esteem human tradition above God's holy truth, Roman Catholics will affirm and teach that Mary is the mother of God so they can elevate her to be more than what the Bible principally teaches. This is commonly called "Mariology," but true Christians call it "myths."

According to Roman Catholicism, Mary is the mother of God, Mary is co-redemptrix or mediatrix, Mary was born and remained sinless (immaculate conception), Mary remained a virgin (perpetual virginity), and Mary ascended body and soul into glory (assumption). These aforementioned doctrines cannot be supported in Scripture.

Thus, the purpose of this chapter is to demonstrate that the Roman Catholic doctrine of Mariology is radically unbiblical because it is nothing more than pagan worship or gross idolatry, which elevates a sinful woman above the Savior's work.

I. "Mother of God"

Holy Scripture teaches that Mary was a godly woman who was saved by God's grace. In the Bible, she is referred to as "highly favored" (Luke 1:28), "the Lord's servant" (Luke 1:38), and "blessed" (Luke 1:48). During the crucifixion, Mary was at the feet of Jesus (John 19:25).

Most notably, the angel told Mary, the virgin, that she had found favor with God "And behold, thou shalt conceive in thy womb, and bring forth a son, and shalt call his name JESUS" (Luke 1:31). As a result, Elisabeth said to Mary, "And whence is this to me, that the mother of my Lord should come to me" (Luke 1:43)?

Even though the Bible says that Mary is the mother of the "Lord" in Luke 1:43, Arians will twist this text to teach that Christ is a created being, and Roman Catholics will also abuse this passage to promote their godless views of Mary in lieu of propagating the merits of Christ alone.

CCC 963: Since the Virgin Mary's role in the mystery of Christ and the Spirit has been treated, it is fitting now to consider her place in the mystery of the Church. "The Virgin Mary . . . is acknowledged and honored as being truly the **Mother of God** and of the redeemer.... She is 'clearly the mother of the members of Christ' ... since she has by her charity joined in bringing about the birth of believers in the Church, who are members of its head." "Mary, Mother of Christ, **Mother of the Church**."

CCC 966: "Finally the Immaculate Virgin, **preserved free from all stain of original sin**, when the course of her earthly life was finished, **was taken up body and soul into heavenly glory**, and **exalted by the Lord as Queen over all things**, so that she might be the more fully conformed to her Son, the Lord of lords and conqueror of sin and death." The Assumption of the Blessed Virgin is a singular participation in her Son's Resurrection and an anticipation of the resurrection of other Christians:

> In giving birth you kept your virginity; in your Dormition you did not leave the world, O **Mother of God**, but were joined to the source of Life. You conceived the living God and, by your prayers, will deliver our souls from death.

. . . she is our Mother in the order of grace

CCC 971: "All generations will call me blessed": **"The Church's devotion to the Blessed Virgin is intrinsic to Christian worship**." The Church rightly honors "the Blessed Virgin with special devotion. From the most ancient times the Blessed Virgin has been honored with the title of **'Mother of God,'** to whose protection the faithful fly in all their dangers and needs.... This very special devotion ... differs essentially from the adoration which is given to the incarnate Word and equally to the Father and the Holy

Spirit, and greatly fosters this adoration." The liturgical feasts dedicated to the Mother of God and Marian prayer, such as the rosary, an "epitome of the whole Gospel," express this devotion to the Virgin Mary.

CCC 975: "We believe that the **Holy Mother of God**, the new Eve, Mother of the Church, continues in heaven to exercise her maternal role on behalf of the members of Christ" (Paul VI, CPG # 15). (emphasis mine)

As shown above, Roman Catholics call Mary the "mother of God" because they believe she is preserved free from all stain of original sin, they believe she was taken up body and soul into heavenly glory, they believe she was exalted by the Lord as Queen over all things, and they believe she is the mother in the order of grace, etc., which are all heretical doctrines that will be addressed in this chapter.

Thus, Christians need to rightly interpret the Bible and explain what mother of the Lord means in Luke 1:43 because Roman Catholics need to be shown that Mariology is synonymous with idolatry.

Historically, a notable heretic named Nestorius once argued that Mary should be called "mother of Christ" [*Christotokos*; Christ-bearer], not "mother of God" [*Theotokos*; God-bearer]. This was due to the fact that Nestorius believed that Christ is two distinct persons or *hypostases* (Nestorian heresy), not one person.

Biblically, Mary is the mother of the Lord, but it is with respect to Jesus' humanity, not His divinity because the preexistent Christ is uncaused, eternally self-existent, and is in every way God, but distinct from the Father. So the only way to interpret Luke 1:43 is to have a biblical understanding of the hypostatic union of Jesus Christ, which teaches that He is simultaneously wholly God and wholly man (two natures), yet one person.

However, in order to understand the hypostatic union of Christ, Christians must examine the following verbs: *ēn* [imperf. "was", John 1] and *egeneto* ["became," John 1:14], *hyparchōn* [part. "being," Philippians 2:6] and *genomenos* [part. "being," Philippians 2:7]. Also contrast the noun *morphē* ["form," Philippians 2:6] with *schēmati* ["fashion," Philippians 2:8].

For example, John 1:1 states, "In the beginning **was** the Word, and the Word **was** with God, and the Word **was** God" (emphasis mine). The highlighted stative verb [Gk: "en"; Eng: "was"] is in the imperfect tense, which indicates "…continuous timeless existence."[39] Additionally, the verb "was" is in all three clauses of John 1, which reveals Christ's preexistence, distinction of persons in the Godhead, and the Son's full deity.

---

[39] Cleon L. Rogers Jr. and Cleon L. Rogers III, *The New Linguistic and Exegetical Key to the Greek New Testament* (Grand Rapids, MI: Zondervan Publishing House, 1998), 175. All subsequent references of Greek definitions will be cited in the following manner: for example, Rogers & Rogers, 1998, 189.

But in John 1:14, the Bible states, "And the Word was **made** flesh, and dwelt among us…" (emphasis mine). The verb *made* indicates that the preexistent Christ, God the Logos, became [Gk: "sarx egeneto"; lit., "to become, be made"] flesh,[40] with respect to His humanity. Thus, Christ has two natures, yet He is one person.

After contrasting the two verbs in John 1:1 ("was") and John 1:14 ("made"), it's evident that Christ is simultaneously wholly God and fully man, which is why He is referred to as the God-Man, or *Theanthropos*. But having two distinct, unmingled, and inseparable natures does not mean that one should believe in a two person Christ; it indicates that Christ's divinity and humanity were indissolubly united in one *hypostasis*, not two (Nestorian heresy).

Nestorian false teachers will argue that not holding to a two-person view leads to Patripassianism or Theopassionism, but that is nonsense. With respect to His humanity, the person of Christ died a substitutionary and propitiatory death for the sheep, not goats. And the person of Christ resurrected for the justification of the elect, not reprobate, in accordance with His divinity. Christ has two inseparable natures, yet He is one person.

---

[40] Joseph H. Thayer, *Thayer's Greek-English Lexicon of the New Testament* (Peabody, MA: Hendrickson Publishers), 115. Reprinted form the fourth edition originally published by T. & T. Clark, Edinburgh, 1896, with *Strong's* numberings added by Hendrickson Publishers.

Bottom line: Mary is the mother of the Lord as stated in Luke 1:43 (with respect to Christ's humanity), but she is not the mother of God per the Roman Catholic traditions, which do not rightfully divide the Word of God.[41]

II. "Co-Redemptrix" or "Mediatrix"

Nonetheless, as previously discussed, Arians and Nestorians are not the only ones who will twist Scripture. Roman Catholics will abuse Luke 1:43 to give unbiblical titles to Mary (i.e., co-redemptrix,

---

[41] See the Chalcedonian Creed, which states: "We, then, following the holy fathers, all with one consent teach men to confess one and the same Son, our Lord Jesus Christ, the same perfect in Godhead and also perfect in manhood; truly God and truly man, of a rational soul and body; coessential with the Father according to the Godhead, and consubstantial with us according to the manhood; in all things like unto us, without sin; begotten before all ages of the Father according to the Godhead, and in these latter days, for us and for our salvation, **born of the Virgin Mary, the mother of God, according to the manhood**; **one and the same Christ, Son, Lord, Only-begotten, to be acknowledged in two natures**, without confusion, without change, without division, without separation; the distinction of natures being by no means taken away by the union, but rather the property of each nature being preserved, and concurring in one person and one subsistence, not parted or divided into two persons, but one and the same Son, and only begotten, God the Word, the Lord Jesus Christ; as the prophets from the beginning have declared concerning Him, and the Lord Jesus Christ Himself has taught us, and the creed of the holy fathers has handed down to us." (emphasis mine)

mediatrix, advocate, helper, etc.),[42] which will now be addressed and refuted in accordance with Scripture.

a. "Co-Redemptrix"

First, referring to Mary as co-redemptrix[43] is heresy because the Father decreed the salvation of the

---

[42] See CCC 969: "This motherhood of Mary in the order of grace continues uninterruptedly from the consent which she loyally gave at the Annunciation and which she sustained without wavering beneath the cross, until the eternal fulfilment of all the elect. Taken up to heaven she did not lay aside this saving office but by her manifold intercession continues to bring us the gifts of eternal salvation .... Therefore **the Blessed Virgin is invoked in the Church under the titles of Advocate, Helper, Benefactress**, and **Mediatrix**." (emphasis mine)

[43] See CCC 494: "At the announcement that she would give birth to "the Son of the Most High" without knowing man, by the power of the Holy Spirit, Mary responded with the obedience of faith, certain that "with God nothing will be impossible": "Behold, I am the handmaid of the Lord; let it be [done] to me according to your word." Thus, giving her consent to God's word, Mary becomes the mother of Jesus. Espousing the divine will for salvation wholeheartedly, without a single sin to restrain her, she gave herself entirely to the person and to the work of her Son; **she did so in order to serve the mystery of redemption with him and dependent on him**, by God's grace: As St. Irenaeus says, "**Being obedient she became the cause of salvation for herself and for the whole human race**." Hence not a few of the early Fathers gladly assert. . .: "The knot of Eve's disobedience was untied by Mary's obedience: what the virgin Eve bound through her disbelief, Mary loosened by her faith." Comparing her with Eve, they call Mary "the Mother of the living" and frequently claim: "**Death through Eve, life through Mary**."" (emphasis mine)

elect in eternity,[44] the Son purchased the sheep,[45] and the Spirit seals God's particular people in due time.[46] Put another way, the elect of God for whom Christ died will be sealed by the Spirit, which means the Triune God alone is the author of redemption, not Mary.

God's word never teaches that Mary, a sinner, plays a part in the salvation of God's elect. Thus, holding to the delirious view that Mary is co-redemptrix denies the biblical doctrine of election, it rejects the sufficiency of particular redemption, and it robs the Triune God of glory. Bottom line: Mary takes no part in the redemption of God's particular people because she is a sinner, not the Savior.

b. "Mediatrix"

Second, referring to Mary as mediatrix is heresy because the Bible teaches that Christ is the

---

[44] **See Ephesians 1:3-6**: "Blessed be the God and Father of our Lord Jesus Christ, who hath blessed us with all spiritual blessings in heavenly places in Christ: According as he hath chosen us in him before the foundation of the world, that we should be holy and without blame before him in love: Having predestinated us unto the adoption of children by Jesus Christ to himself, according to the good pleasure of his will, To the praise of the glory of his grace, wherein he hath made us accepted in the beloved."

[45] See Ephesians 1:7: "In whom we have redemption through his blood, the forgiveness of sins, according to the riches of his grace."

[46] See Ephesians 1:13: "In whom ye also trusted, after that ye heard the word of truth, the gospel of your salvation: in whom also after that ye believed, ye were sealed with that holy Spirit of promise."

only mediator. First Timothy 2:5 states, "For there is one God, and **one mediator** between God and men, the man Christ Jesus" (emphasis mine). As a result, arguing that Mary should be referred to as mediatrix is tantamount to defiantly making it known that one stands with Catholicism, not Christ.

c. "Advocate" or "Helper"

Third, according to Roman Catholic tradition, Mary is called "advocate" and "helper," but God's Word teaches that the Holy Spirit is the advocate and helper. John 14:26 states, "But the **Comforter**, which is the Holy Ghost, whom the Father will send in my name, he shall teach you all things, and bring all things to your remembrance, whatsoever I have said unto you" (emphasis mine).

Since Roman Catholics refer to Mary with titles that belong to the Holy Spirit, they are faced with yet another dilemma, which always reveals that their traditions are contrary to the Word of God. The Holy Spirit is the advocate and helper of God's elect, not Mary, because only the third person of the Trinity will guide the sheep into all truth (John 16:13).

Therefore, when Roman Catholics ascribe unbiblical titles to a sinner, they are sending a message to everyone that they worship Mary, not the Master, which can be seen in CCC 971: "…The Church's devotion to the Blessed Virgin is intrinsic to Christian worship."

However, Roman Catholics will argue that they worship God alone, not Mary. Review the following excerpts below to see how one scholar explained that Roman Catholics rely on subterfuge or sophistry to exonerate themselves of idolatry:

> …to avoid the charge of worshiping Mary (in the same sense as worshiping God), the RCC has developed (again, throughout the years) a doctrinal scheme that distinguishes two kinds of worship: latria (Gk. latreia) meaning, "honor," which is to God alone and dulia (Gk. duleia) meaning, "servitude" (veneration), which is given to the saints; however, Mary is to receive "hyper-dulia," which is the highest form of dulia. In this way, Catholics can avert the charge of idolatry when they pray to Mary and the saints and bow before statues while reciting the Rosary.

> But is this distinction of between latria and dulia biblically valid? Does Scripture permit and even teach that Christians should give dulia to creatures and hyperdulia to Mary in a religious context? Absolutely not! Praying to Mary (and the saints) bowing before statues of her, giving her "hyperdulia" is pure idolatry, hence, creaturely worship. Note the following:

> …Three forms of the same thing–which is functional "worship: latria, which is the highest form of worship—reserved for God alone, dulia, which is given to saints, and hyperdulia (the highest form of dulia), which is given to Mary…

...Regarding idols and false gods, God commands in Exodus 20:5: "You shall not worship them or serve them; for I the LORD your God, am a jealous God." The term translated "serve" is from the Hebrew word abad. The "most frequent English translation of the term is 'to serve.'" In fact, both "to serve" and "worship" are translated from the same word, abad in many places in the OT. Further, the Septuagint (LXX) translates abad as both douleuō/duleia and latreuō/latreia. Thus, there no distinction made between the terms in the context of religious worship—to give dulia is to give latria.

In Galatians 4:8, Paul says, "when you did not know God, you were slaves to those which by nature are no gods." The phrase "were slaves" (or "you served") is from the verb douleuō. Paul was clear: "to serve" (i.e., to give dulia) anyone other than God in a religious context is wrong—it is idolatry.[47]

III. Immaculate Conception

Another heresy taught by the Roman Catholic tradition is the immaculate conception. This doctrine basically teaches that Mary was conceived without sin, and she was "preserved immune from all stain of

---

[47] Dalcour, E. (2018, February 8). *A Concise look at Roman Catholicism and the Functional worship of Mary*. Department of Christian Defense. Retrieved July 14, 2022, from https://christiandefense.org/roman-catholicism/a-concise-look-at-roman-catholicism-and-the-functional-worship-of-mary/

original sin." God's Word teaches that all created beings are born in sin and thus have a sinful nature, but Roman Catholicism teaches that Mary, a created being, was born sinless and never sinned in her life:

> CCC 490: To become the mother of the Saviour, Mary "was enriched by God with gifts appropriate to such a role." The angel Gabriel at the moment of the annunciation salutes her as "full of grace". In fact, in order for Mary to be able to give the free assent of her faith to the announcement of her vocation, it was necessary that she be wholly borne by God's grace.

> CCC 491: Through the centuries the Church has become ever more aware that Mary, "full of grace" through God, **was redeemed from the moment of her conception**. That is what the dogma of the Immaculate Conception confesses, as Pope Pius IX proclaimed in 1854:

> > The most Blessed Virgin Mary was, from the first moment of her conception, by a singular grace and privilege of almighty God and by virtue of the merits of Jesus Christ, Saviour of the human race, **preserved immune from all stain of original sin**.

> CCC 492: The "splendour of an entirely unique holiness" by which Mary is "**enriched from the first instant of her conception**"

comes wholly from Christ: she is "redeemed, in a more exalted fashion, by reason of the merits of her Son". The Father blessed Mary more than any other created person "in Christ with every spiritual blessing in the heavenly places" and chose her "in Christ before the foundation of the world, to be holy and blameless before him in love".

CCC 493: The Fathers of the Eastern tradition call the Mother of God "the All-Holy" (Panagia), and celebrate her as "**free from any stain of sin**, as though fashioned by the Holy Spirit and formed as a new creature". **By the grace of God Mary remained free of every personal sin her whole life long**. "Let it be done to me according to your word. . ."

CCC 494: At the announcement that she would give birth to "the Son of the Most High" without knowing man, by the power of the Holy Spirit, Mary responded with the obedience of faith, certain that "with God nothing will be impossible": "Behold, I am the handmaid of the Lord; let it be [done] to me according to your word." Thus, giving her consent to God's word, Mary becomes the mother of Jesus. Espousing the divine will for salvation wholeheartedly, **without a single sin to restrain her**, she gave herself entirely to the person and to the work of her Son; she did so in order to serve the mystery of redemption with him and dependent on him, by God's grace:

As St. Irenaeus says, "Being obedient
she became the cause of salvation for
herself and for the whole human race."
Hence not a few of the early Fathers
gladly assert. . .: "The knot of Eve's
disobedience was untied by Mary's
obedience: what the virgin Eve bound
through her disbelief, Mary loosened
by her faith." Comparing her with Eve,
they call Mary "the Mother of the
living" and frequently claim: "Death
through Eve, life through Mary."
(emphasis mine)

Regarding the so-called immaculate
conception, the Bible never teaches or even implies
that Mary was born sinless, and remained sinless her
whole life. In fact, God's Word teaches that all have
sinned (Romans 3:23)[48] because Adam's sin was
imputed to the entire human race after the fall.[49] See
Turretin's arguments on why Mary was not sinless:

She herself had need of a Savior, whom she
celebrates as hers (Lk. 1:47). She was bound
to offer the sacrifices of the old law, which
could not be done without the confession of
sin. The effects of that sin are found in her, as
are actual sins. On account of this, we read
that she was rebuked even by Christ (Jn. 2:4;

____

[48] This passage states, "For all have sinned, and come
short of the glory of God."

[49] See Romans 5:12: "Wherefore, as by one man sin
entered into the world, and death by sin; and so death passed
upon all men, for that **all have sinned**" (emphasis mine).

Lk. 2:49; 8:19-21), calamity and trials (which are the fruits of sin) piercing through her soul (Lk. 2:35).[50]

Turretin's argument is sound. The Bible teaches that Mary knew she was a sinner because she rejoiced in her Savior in Luke 1:47, when she said, "And my spirit hath rejoiced in God my Saviour." Mary also knew she was a sinner due to the fact that she offered sacrifices in accordance with the law (Luke 2:24),[51] which was a "sin offering" (Leviticus 12:8).[52] Thus, the Roman Catholic doctrine of the immaculate conception is based on fiction, not fact.

IV. Perpetual Virginity

Roman Catholics also confess Mary's real and perpetual virginity. What does this mean? The Bible teaches that Mary was a virgin (Isaiah 7:14; Matthew 1:23; Luke 1:27), but God's Word clearly teaches that she did not remain a virgin. However, Roman Catholics believe in Mary's so-called real and perpetual virginity, which can be seen below:

CCC 499: The deepening of faith in the virginal motherhood led the Church to confess

---

[50] Turretin, 1:635.

[51] This passage states, "And to offer a sacrifice according to that which is said in the law of the Lord, A pair of turtledoves, or two young pigeons."

[52] This passage states, "And if she be not able to bring a lamb, then she shall bring two turtles, or two young pigeons; the one for the burnt offering, and the other for a sin offering: and the priest shall make an atonement for her, and she shall be clean."

Mary's real and perpetual virginity even in the act of giving birth to the Son of God made man. In fact, Christ's birth "did not diminish his mother's virginal integrity but sanctified it." and so the liturgy of the Church celebrates Mary as Aeiparthenos, the "Ever-virgin".

CCC 500: Against this doctrine the objection is sometimes raised that the Bible mentions brothers and sisters of Jesus. The Church has always understood these passages as not referring to other children of the Virgin Mary. In fact James and Joseph, "brothers of Jesus", are the sons of another Mary, a disciple of Christ, whom St. Matthew significantly calls "the other Mary". They are close relations of Jesus, according to an Old Testament expression.

CCC 501: Jesus is Mary's only son, but her spiritual motherhood extends to all men whom indeed he came to save: "The Son whom she brought forth is he whom God placed as the first-born among many brethren, that is, the faithful in whose generation and formation she co-operates with a mother's love." (emphasis mine).

Regarding the so-called doctrine of perpetual virginity, Richard Bennett provided an exhaustive analysis of Mary's real marriage and Christ's siblings, which refutes Roman Catholic tradition (CCC 499-501):

This "ever Virgin" role allotted to Mary by the Catholic Church is not Scriptural. There are several passages that mention the brothers and sisters of Christ Jesus. An example is found in Mark's gospel, "*Is this not the carpenter, the Son of Mary, and the brother of James, Joses, Judas, and Simon? And are not His sisters here with us?*" (Mark 6:3) Another is found in Matthew's gospel account, "*Is this not the carpenter's son? Is not His mother called Mary? and His brothers James, Joses, Simon, and Judas? And His sisters, are they not all with us?*" (Matthew 13:55-56) From these and other texts, it is clear that Jesus had brothers and sisters. The Holy Spirit as the author of all Scripture used the precise language of Greek in which there is a clear distinction between brother "adelphos" (literally, "a" meaning "from," and "delphus" meaning "womb") and nephew "anepsios" a cousin, or sister's son. Likewise, the Apostle Paul, under the inspiration Holy Spirit calls James "the Lord's brother." (Galatians 3:16) The word he used in the Greek is "adelphos" meaning brother rather than "anepsios," signifying cousin. The Holy Spirit again in the Gospel of Mark is utterly precise in using the distinct word for brother, "*Is not this the carpenter, the son of Mary, the brother [adelphos] of James.*" (Mark 6:3)

While "adelphos" is employed on occasion in some writings in the New Testament to refer to the larger company of believers and disciples, the context of the passages in Mark and Matthew are such that anything other than the literal sense would involve an absurdity. "Brothers and sisters" signifying believers and disciples would be bizarre in the context. To claim the concept of "cousins" is equally ruled out; as such meaning is always given as "anepsioi" to signify that relationship. The Holy Spirit clearly states not only that Christ Jesus had siblings, but also in the gospel of John, He distinguishes between siblings and disciples, "…*He [the Lord], and His mother and His brethren and His disciples*…." (John 2:12)

In another and seemingly desperate attempt to preserve the tradition that Mary remained forever a virgin, the Church of Rome proposes that in the Scripture accounts, brothers and sisters of Jesus refer to another Mary. Thus it is stated,

"Against this doctrine the objection is sometimes raised that the Bible mentions brothers and sisters of Jesus. The Church has always understood these passages as not referring to other children of the Virgin Mary. In fact James and Joseph, 'brothers of Jesus', are the sons of another Mary, a disciple of Christ, whom St. Matthew significantly calls 'the other Mary'. They are close relations of Jesus, according to an Old Testament expression." (CCC 500)

Another Mary? Why the twisting of Scripture? These verses clearly refer to "…*His mother called Mary? and His brothers James, Joses, Simon, and Judas*?" (Matthew 13:55) So why does the Catholic Church deliberately mislead its members? It is to propagate an image of Mary as a quasi-divine creature, who is above having a normal marital relationship with her husband, Joseph, and to establish her as a role model for nuns and priests to live a celibate life.

The doctrine of the virginity of Mary before the birth of Jesus is a doctrine of the Scriptures that is a very important part of Biblical faith. But the Scriptures do not teach the perpetual virginity of Mary; in fact it teaches the opposite. Marriage is commended and called honorable on the pages of Scripture. Who was more highly favored than Mary was in her marriage? Thus the Scripture teaches, *"when as his mother Mary was espoused to Joseph, before they came together, she was found with child of the Holy Ghost."* (Matthew 1:18) The term "came together" includes the idea of sexual intimacy. The implication clearly is that ultimately Mary and Joseph indeed "came together." Then the Scripture states, *"then Joseph… took to him his wife, and did not know her till she had brought forth her firstborn Son. And he called His name Jesus."* (Matthew 1:24-25) The language here makes it clear that she lived as the virgin wife of Joseph until Christ Jesus was born. Joseph did not know her sexually prior to that birth. Neither the word "till" nor "firstborn" necessarily specifies what happened afterward. However, one would naturally infer that the normal relationship of marriage would follow, unless one is committed to defend the tradition of the perpetual virginity of Mary. The Holy Spirit through the writing of Matthew reveals no such inclination.[53]

V. Assumption of Mary

Another way Roman Catholics exalt Mary, a sinner saved by grace, is by asserting that she ascended into heavenly glory. The Bible does teach that Elijah was taken up by a whirlwind into heaven. Second Kings 2:11 states, "And it came to pass, as they still went on, and talked, that, behold, there appeared a chariot of fire, and horses of fire, and parted them both asunder; and Elijah went up by a whirlwind into heaven." But the Bible does not say that Mary's body and soul were taken up to heaven.

Additionally, Roman Catholics not only believe Mary ascended into heavenly glory, which the Bible does not state, they also think that the Lord has exalted her as "Queen" over all things, which is blasphemy.

CCC 966: "Finally the Immaculate Virgin, preserved free from all stain of original sin, when the course of her earthly life was

---

[53] Bennett, R. (n.d.). *The Biblical Mary Vs. Rome's Counterfeit Mary*. Burean Beacon. Retrieved July 15, 2022, from https://bereanbeacon.org/the-biblical-mary-vs-romes-counterfeit-mary/#_edn15.

finished, **was taken up body and soul into heavenly glory, and exalted by the Lord as Queen over all things**, so that she might be the more fully conformed to her Son, the Lord of lords and conqueror of sin and death." The Assumption of the Blessed Virgin is a singular participation in her Son's Resurrection and an anticipation of the resurrection of other Christians:

> In giving birth you kept your virginity; in your Dormition you did not leave the world, O Mother of God, but were joined to the source of Life. You conceived the living God and, by your prayers, will deliver our souls from death.

. . . she is our Mother in the order of grace

CCC 974: The Most Blessed Virgin Mary, when the course of her earthly life was completed, **was taken up body and soul into the glory of heaven**, where she already shares in the glory of her Son's Resurrection, anticipating the resurrection of all members of his Body.

The aforementioned catechisms are absurd because asserting that Mary was taken up body and soul into heavenly glory and exalted as "Queen" over all things are contrary to the Word of God. Richard Bennett argued that the so-called assumption of Mary doctrine is nothing more than an unbiblical tradition:

…This is truly an absurd dogma since there is no Scriptural mention of it and there was not even any early tradition on the subject. Roman Catholic scholars such as Ludwig Ott admit this when he states,

"The idea of the bodily assumption of Mary is first expressed in certain transitus–narratives of the fifth and sixth centuries. Even though these are apocryphal they bear witness to the faith of the generation in which they were written despite their legendary clothing. The first Church author to speak of the bodily ascension of Mary, in association with an apocryphal transitus B.M.V., is St. Gregory of Tours +594."

…Besides the official teaching of the assumption, the same assumed Mary is proclaimed "Queen over all things." For the Catholics, the popular prayer following the Rosary is the "Hail Holy Queen." It starts, "Hail Holy Queen, mother of mercy, hail our life, our sweetness and our hope." This is the offering of one's life and hope to the Queen of Heaven. The official litany of the Roman Mary calls her, "Queen of Angels, Queen of Patriarchs, Queen of Prophets, Queen of Apostles, Queen of Martyrs, Queen of Confessors, Queen of Virgins, Queen of all Saints, Queen conceived without original sin, Queen assumed into heaven, Queen of the most holy Rosary, Queen of Peace."

This is quite similar to what the perverse Israelites did in Old Testament times as recorded by the Prophet Jeremiah, *"The children gather wood, and the fathers kindle the fire, and the women knead their dough, to make cakes to the queen of heaven, and to pour out drink offerings unto other gods, that they may provoke me to anger."* (Jeremiah 7:18)

…In chapters four and five of the Book of Revelation, a quite detailed picture of Heaven is given. God is seated on the throne, surrounded by twenty-four elders and four living creatures. The Lamb, the Lord Christ Jesus, is on the throne. Many thousands of angels circle the throne, singing God's praises. There is no Queen of Heaven, for such would be an abomination to the Lord. The Lord God alone is glorified. *"Look to me, and be ye saved, all the ends of the earth: for I am God, and there is none else."* (Isaiah 45:22) Those who promote such worship to the Queen of Heaven *"shall drink of the wine of the wrath of God, which is poured out without mixture into the cup of his indignation."* (Revelation 14:10)[54]

VI. Closing

This chapter has demonstrated that Mariology is radically unbiblical. Thus, referring to Mary with titles that belong to God is blasphemous, not biblical.

---

[54] Ibid.

Asserting that Mary was born without sin and remained sinless is based on godless traditions, not the gospel. And maintaining the belief in Mary's so-called real and perpetual virginity and assumption are imbecilic opinions, not inspired biblical truths.

STUDY QUESTIONS

1. If you know Roman Catholics, what are some of their beliefs about Mary?

2. What does the Bible teach about Mary?

3. How will Arians twist Luke 1:43?

4. How do Roman Catholics abuse Luke 1:43?

5. Why do Roman Catholics call Mary "mother of God?"

6. According to this chapter, Mariology is synonymous with what?

7. What is the hypostatic union of Christ?

8. The only way to interpret Luke 1:43 is to have a biblical understanding of what?

9. What unbiblical titles do Roman Catholics ascribe to Mary?

10. What is the problem with arguing that Mary is co-redemptrix?

11. Is Mary a mediator between God and man?

12. Read 1 Timothy 2:5 and explain how this passage refutes Mariology.

13. According to the Bible, who is the advocate and helper?

14. When Roman Catholics ascribe unbiblical titles to Mary, they are sending a message to everyone that they worship whom?

15. What is the doctrine of immaculate conception?

16. Does the Bible teach that Mary was born sinless and preserved immune from all stain of original sin?

17. Read Turretin's excerpt on why Mary was not sinless and explain how this has helped you to refute the doctrine of immaculate conception.

18. Do Roman Catholics believe in Mary's so-called real and perpetual virginity?

19. Explain how Richard Bennett refuted the Roman Catholic doctrine of perpetual virginity.

20. According to the Bible, who was taken up body and soul into heaven?

21. Does the Bible ever teach that Mary ascended body and soul into heaven?

22. Read CCC 966 and explain why Richard Bennett regarded this as heresy.

23. After reading this chapter, explain in one word what you think about Mariology.

24. How would you share the gospel with a Roman Catholic who believes in Mariology?

25. Do you pray for Roman Catholics who affirm Mariology?

CHAPTER 4

DEFY ROME'S FALSE GOSPEL

Roman Catholicism is a worldview that depends heavily on godless traditions,[55] not gospel truths. So affirming Roman Catholicism is no different than denying salvation by grace alone through faith alone in Christ alone. Thus, one can easily deduce that Roman Catholic dogmas derive from hell, not heaven.

As stated in the previous chapters, the pope is anti-Christian, and Roman Catholic dogmas are anti-gospel, which means Roman Catholicism is synonymous with blasphemy and idolatry. Nonetheless, there is a proliferation of Roman Catholics who will side with Catholicism, not Christ,[56] by affirming the following:

- Roman Catholics think the source of justification is one's fictitious free will, not the Father's free grace.

---

[55] Paul warned about the dangers of human tradition in Colossians 2:8. This text states, "Beware lest any man spoil you through philosophy and vain deceit, **after the tradition of men**, after the rudiments of the world, and not after Christ" (emphasis mine).

[56] There is no such thing as neutrality in Scripture. In Matthew 12:30, Christ said, "He that is not with me is against me; and he that gathereth not with me scattereth abroad." Therefore, those who dignify Roman Catholicism deny Christ's righteousness.

- Roman Catholics will argue that a believer's soul is cleansed by the sacrament of baptism, not the Savior's blood.

- Roman Catholics believe salvation points to their attendance or membership in church, not the merits of Christ alone.

- Roman Catholics elevate their so-called good works above God's will.

- Roman Catholics will posit that salvation is grounded in the law, regulations, or accomplishments, not the Lord's righteousness alone.

The purpose of this chapter is to examine and give a rebuttal of several Roman Catholic dogmas, which clearly reject the doctrine of salvation by particular grace alone (source of justification) through faith alone (alone instrument) in the righteousness of Christ alone (ground of justification).

I. Roman Catholicism teaches that a fallible sinner can merit God's free grace.

CCC 2010: Since the initiative belongs to God in the order of grace, no one can merit the initial grace of forgiveness and justification, at the beginning of conversion. Moved by the Holy Spirit and by charity, **we can then merit for ourselves and for others the graces needed for our sanctification, for the increase of grace and charity, and for the**

attainment of eternal life. Even temporal goods like health and friendship can be merited in accordance with God's wisdom. These graces and goods are the object of Christian prayer. Prayer attends to the grace we need for meritorious actions. (emphasis mine)

Biblical Response: Roman Catholics rely on sophistry, not Scripture, when discussing theological matters. God's Word never teaches that fallible sinners can merit the grace of God that is needed for eternal life. In fact, the Bible never teaches that human beings can merit anything from God.[57] This is why one notable theologian argued that the only thing a sinner can merit with God is His wrath.

Scripture teaches that grace and works do not mix. This is due to the fact that grace and works are diametrically opposed. For example, in Romans 4, the apostle Paul said, "Now to him that worketh is the reward not reckoned of grace, but of debt. But to him that worketh not, but believeth on him that justifieth the ungodly, his faith is counted for righteousness" (vv. 4-5).

Additionally, it's impossible to argue that one can merit God's grace because the Bible teaches that God's grace, biblically defined, is free and

---

[57] Asserting that one can merit God's favor is tantamount to saying that one can be saved by grace and works. But Paul said, "For by grace are ye saved through faith; and that **not of yourselves**: it is the gift of God: **Not of works**, lest any man should boast" (Ephesians 2:8-9, emphasis mine).

undeserved. Romans 11:6 states, "And if by grace, then is it no more of works: otherwise grace is no more grace. But if it be of works, then it is no more grace: otherwise work is no more work."

Moreover, asserting that one can merit God's favor is tantamount to denying the sovereignty of God in the salvation or condemnation of sinners.[58] According to Scripture, God actively chose the elect, and He actively reprobated the wicked. Thus, God loves the elect, and hates the wicked.

The Bible teaches that God loved Jacob, but hated Esau, and it was before they were even born, which means no one can merit God's favor because the Lord does as He pleases in the salvation or condemnation of sinners. See Romans 9:11-13:

(For the children being not yet born, neither having done any good or evil, that the purpose of God according to election might stand, not of works, but of him that calleth;) It was said unto her, The elder shall serve the younger. As

---

[58] Psalm 115:3 states, "But our God is in the heavens: he hath done whatsoever he hath pleased." Many will disagree with this passage. But Paul sets the record straight in Romans 9:19-23: "Thou wilt say then unto me, Why doth he yet find fault? For who hath resisted his will? Nay but, O man, who art thou that repliest against God? Shall the thing formed say to him that formed it, Why hast thou made me thus? Hath not the potter power over the clay, of the same lump to make one vessel unto honour, and another unto dishonour? What if God, willing to shew his wrath, and to make his power known, endured with much longsuffering the vessels of wrath fitted to destruction: And that he might make known the riches of his glory on the vessels of mercy, which he had afore prepared unto glory."

it is written, Jacob have I loved, but Esau have I hated.

II. Roman Catholicism teaches that water baptism is necessary for salvation.

CCC 1257: **The Lord himself affirms that Baptism is necessary for salvation**. He also commands his disciples to proclaim the Gospel to all nations and to baptize them. Baptism is necessary for salvation for those to whom the Gospel has been proclaimed and who have had the possibility of asking for this sacrament. The Church does not know of any means other than Baptism that assures entry into eternal beatitude; this is why she takes care not to neglect the mission she has received from the Lord to see that all who can be baptized are "reborn of water and the Spirit." **God has bound salvation to the sacrament of Baptism**, but he himself is not bound by his sacraments. (emphasis mine)

Biblical Response: Arguing that water baptism is absolutely necessary for salvation is a notable heresy called "baptismal regeneration." According to papists, water baptism can transform a dead sinner into a delivered saint, and water baptism can make a child of wrath into a child of God. This is due to the fact that false teachers hold to baptismal regeneration in accordance with Catholicism, not biblical redemption in Christ alone.

But according to Scripture, the elect of God were justified by the blood of Christ, the saints have

forgiveness through the blood of Christ, God's
particular people have peace through the blood of
Christ, the sheep were redeemed by the blood of
Christ, and those for whom Christ died know their
sins were washed by the the Savior's blood, not a
baptismal ceremony.

> **Acts 20:28**: "Take heed therefore unto
> yourselves, and to all the flock, over the which
> the Holy Ghost hath made you overseers, to
> feed the church of God, which he hath
> purchased with his own blood."

> **Romans 5:9**: "Much more then, being now
> justified by his blood, we shall be saved from
> wrath through him."

> **Ephesians 1:7**: "In whom we have
> redemption through his blood, the forgiveness
> of sins, according to the riches of his grace."

> **Colossians 1:20**: "And, having made peace
> through the blood of his cross, by him to
> reconcile all things unto himself; by him, I
> say, whether they be things in earth, or things
> in heaven."

> **Hebrews 9:14**: "How much more shall the
> blood of Christ, who through the eternal Spirit
> offered himself without spot to God, purge
> your conscience from dead works to serve the
> living God?"

> **1 Peter 1:18-19**: "Forasmuch as ye know that
> ye were not redeemed with corruptible things,

as silver and gold, from your vain
conversation received by tradition from your
fathers; But with the precious blood of Christ,
as of a lamb without blemish and without
spot."

Revelation 1:5: "And from Jesus Christ, who
is the faithful witness, and the first begotten of
the dead, and the prince of the kings of the
earth. Unto him that loved us, and washed us
from our sins in his own blood."

**III. Roman Catholicism teaches that membership
in a Roman Catholic Church is a condition of
salvation.**

CCC 845: To reunite all his children, scattered
and led astray by sin, the Father willed to call
the whole of humanity together into his Son's
Church. the Church is the place where
humanity must rediscover its unity and
salvation. the Church is "the world
reconciled." She is that bark which "in the full
sail of the Lord's cross, by the breath of the
Holy Spirit, navigates safely in this world."
According to another image dear to the
Church Fathers, she is prefigured by Noah's
ark, which alone saves from the flood.

CCC 846: How are we to understand this
affirmation, often repeated by the Church
Fathers? Re-formulated positively, **it means
that all salvation comes from Christ the
Head through the Church which is his
Body**:

Basing itself on Scripture and Tradition, **the Council teaches that the Church**, **a pilgrim now on earth**, **is necessary for salvation**: the one Christ is the mediator and the way of salvation; he is present to us in his body which is the Church. He himself explicitly asserted the necessity of faith and Baptism, **and thereby affirmed at the same time the necessity of the Church which men enter through Baptism as through a door**. Hence they could not be saved who, knowing that the Catholic Church was founded as necessary by God through Christ, would refuse either to enter it or to remain in it. (emphasis mine)

Biblical Response: As noted above, Roman Catholicism teaches that salvation is conditional or the basis of salvation points to one's attendance or church membership, not the merits of Christ alone. Also, CCC 845-846 teaches that salvation comes only through the Roman Catholic Church. This conditional view of salvation means the ground of salvation comes from being a devoted member of a Roman Catholic assembly, which is heresy.

Church membership is important, but it's not a condition of salvation. There are several indications of church membership in the Bible. For example, God's Word teaches that the "… the Lord added to the church daily" (Acts 2:47), the Bible teaches that no ones else dared to "…join them" (Acts 5:13), and

Scripture teaches that Christians are to judge those inside the church, but God judges those who are outside the church (1 Corinthians 5:12-13).[59]

However, conflating important doctrines with salvific truths is dangerous, and it is a false gospel. For example, water baptism is important, since it is the great commission (Matthew 28:19). However, water baptism cannot be salvific because the only proper recipients for baptism are those who have already been saved.[60] This means baptism does not save, but only signifies one's identification with Christ's death, burial, and resurrection.

Bottom line: The Bible never teaches that salvation is conditional or that joining a church is a prerequisite to be saved.[61] The completed and saving

---

[59] Also, 2 Corinthians 2:6 references "majority," which indicates that church membership is biblical.

[60] Acts 8 does not teach that the eunuch was saved because of water baptism. The eunuch was not baptized until after Phillip preached the gospel of Christ to him and he professed faith in Christ. Acts 8:35-38 states, "Then Philip opened his mouth, and began at the same scripture, **and preached unto him Jesus**. And as they went on their way, they came unto a certain water: and the eunuch said, See, here is water; what doth hinder me to be baptized? And Philip said, If thou believest with all thine heart, thou mayest. And he answered and said, **I believe that Jesus Christ is the Son of God**. And he commanded the chariot to stand still: and they went down both into the water, both Philip and the eunuch; **and he baptized him**" (emphasis mine).

[61] Acts 4:12 refutes CCC 845-846 because it states, "Neither is there salvation in any other: for there is none other name under heaven given among men, whereby we must be saved." The Bible never teaches that God justifies on the basis of one's membership in a church. On the contrary, Romans 3:24-25

work of Christ or His imputed righteousness is the only ground and assurance of salvation.[62] False teachers like the pope will disagree, but he is a Roman Catholic papist, not a preacher of Christ's righteousness.

IV. Roman Catholicism teaches that good works and law-keeping save.

CCC 1821: We can therefore hope in the glory of heaven promised by God to those who love him and do his will. In every circumstance, each one of us should hope, with the grace of God, to persevere "to the end" and to obtain the joy of heaven, **as God's eternal reward for the good works accomplished with the grace of Christ**. In hope, the Church prays for "all men to be saved." She longs to be united with Christ, her Bridegroom, in the glory of heaven:

CCC 2068: The Council of Trent teaches that the Ten Commandments are obligatory for Christians and that the justified man is still bound to keep them; the Second Vatican Council confirms: "The bishops, successors of

---

states, "**Being justified freely by his grace through the redemption that is in Christ Jesus**: Whom God hath set forth to be a propitiation through faith in his blood, to declare his righteousness for the remission of sins that are past, through the forbearance of God."

[62] See Jeremiah 23:6. This passage states, "In his days Judah shall be saved, and Israel shall dwell safely: and this is his name whereby he shall be called, **THE LORD OUR RIGHTEOUSNESS**" (emphasis mine).

the apostles, receive from the Lord . . . the mission of teaching all peoples, and of preaching the Gospel to every creature, so that all men may attain salvation through faith, Baptism and the **observance of the Commandments**." (emphasis mine)

Biblical Response: Romans Catholics think good works save, but the Bible says that their best works are as "filthy rags" in the sight of God.[63] Put another way, Roman Catholics look to corrupt and fallible works that cannot save, not the finished work of the Savior.

Roman Catholics superstitiously think they can attain salvation by keeping the law,[64] but the Bible teaches Abraham was saved several hundred years before the law. According to Genesis 15:6, "And he believed in the LORD; and he counted it to him for righteousness."

So when Roman Catholics argue that good works or law-keeping saves, they are sending a message that they are deluded sinners, not delivered

---

[63] Isaiah 64:6 states, "But we are all as an unclean thing, **and all our righteousnesses are as filthy rags**; and we all do fade as a leaf; and our iniquities, like the wind, have taken us away" (emphasis mine).

[64] As a disclaimer, sinners cannot keep the law perfectly, sinners who break one law are guilty of breaking them all, sinners who rely on the law as a means of salvation are cursed, unless God delivers them, and God's elect are under grace, not the law. Additionally, law-keeping is not the ground of justification; nor does it provide assurance of salvation.

saints, because the Bible teaches that law-keeping and works do not and will never save.

> **Romans 3:20**: "Therefore by the deeds of the law there shall no flesh be justified in his sight: for by the law is the knowledge of sin."

> **Romans 3:28**: "Therefore we conclude that a man is justified by faith without the deeds of the law."

> **Romans 9:16**: "So then it is not of him that willeth, nor of him that runneth, but of God that sheweth mercy."

> **Romans 9:30-33**: "What shall we say then? That the Gentiles, which followed not after righteousness, have attained to righteousness, even the righteousness which is of faith. But Israel, which followed after the law of righteousness, hath not attained to the law of righteousness. Wherefore? Because they sought it not by faith, but as it were by the works of the law. For they stumbled at that stumblingstone; As it is written, Behold, I lay in Sion a stumblingstone and rock of offence: and whosoever believeth on him shall not be ashamed."

> **Galatians 2:16**: "Knowing that a man is not justified by the works of the law, but by the faith of Jesus Christ, even we have believed in Jesus Christ, that we might be justified by the faith of Christ, and not by the works of the

law: for by the works of the law shall no flesh
be justified."

Galatians 3:10-11: "For as many as are of the
works of the law are under the curse: for it is
written, Cursed is every one that continueth
not in all things which are written in the book
of the law to do them. But that no man is
justified by the law in the sight of God, it is
evident: for, The just shall live by faith."

Galatians 5:4: "Christ is become of no effect
unto you, whosoever of you are justified by
the law; ye are fallen from grace."

Ephesians 2:8-9: "For by grace are ye saved
through faith; and that not of yourselves: it is
the gift of God: Not of works, lest any man
should boast."

2 Timothy 1:9: "Who hath saved us, and
called us with an holy calling, not according
to our works, but according to his own
purpose and grace, which was given us in
Christ Jesus before the world began."

**V. The biblical gospel is the only cure for Roman
Catholics.**

Fake Christians think the only way to reach
Roman Catholics is by establishing a relationship or
by seeking neutrality with them, which is commonly
referred to as *friendship evangelism*. Arguing that
one's friendship with lost people must precede
evangelism is ridiculous, and not biblical. The only

cure for Roman Catholics is the gospel, which is grounded in the Trinity, and is the power of God unto salvation (Romans 1:16).

True Christians worship the one true God (Deuteronomy 6:4), not three independent divine beings, and true Christians know the one true God is multi-personal (Matthew 28:19), not unipersonal. Put another way, the one true God of the Bible exists in a Trinity or plurality of distinct persons who are co-equal, co-eternal, and co-glorious.

As a disclaimer, the Father is not ontologically greater than the Son, the Son is not eternally subordinate to the Father, the Spirit is not inferior to the Father or the Son, and one person is not more glorious than the other persons in the Godhead. All three persons—the Father, the Son, and the Spirit—must be equally worshiped and served (Isaiah 42:8).

Regarding the work of the Triune God in the salvation of sinners, the elect of God for whom Christ died will be sealed by the Spirit (Ephesians 1:3-13). Put another way, the Father ordained or decreed the justification of the elect in eternity, the sins of the elect were imputed to Jesus at the cross, and Christ died for the sheep, not goats. And the Spirit applies regeneration to the elect in time.

The Father is the author of justification (Romans 1:17; 3:24), and He does not declare a sinner to be righteous because He foresaw who would accept or deny Him. God unconditionally and actively chose the elect for heaven and the reprobate for hell, in accordance with His immutable will and sovereignty (Romans 9:11-13). Therefore, God only loves the elect (Romans 5:8; 8:39), and He hates the wicked (Psalm 5:5; 11:5).

God's grace (*Sola Gratia*) is the source of justification (Romans 3:24). But the Bible does not teach that God's grace is prevenient, universal, resistible, or common; nor does the Bible say that one can merit God's grace. According to Scripture, God's grace is discriminative, free, efficacious, irresistible, absolute, and reserved exclusively for the elect of God for whom Christ died.

Christ's righteousness (*Solus Christus*) is the only ground of justification. Adam broke the law, and incurred upon himself and all of his posterity the penalty of sin and death (Romans 5:12). But Christ perfectly obeyed the law (alien preceptive or active obedience), and He died a substitutionary and propitiatory death for the elect (penal or passive obedience), which is the whole work of the righteousness of Christ in its compact unity.

According to the Bible, Christ did not die for all men, His death did not make men savable, His death is not conditioned on fallible men accepting it and applying it to themselves, and it is not a well-meant offer. Christ died for the elect, and He actually redeemed His sheep (Ephesians 1:7) from the curse of the law (Galatians 3:13), and the power of Satan (Hebrews 2:14). Christ propitiated the Father's wrath on behalf of the sheep (1 John 2:2), and the gospel is the power of God to the elect, but foolishness to reprobates (1 Corinthians 1:18).

Adam's sin was imputed to all men without exception, which is why all men are born into this world totally depraved or desperately wicked as can be (Genesis 6:5; Jeremiah 17:9). But God loves the elect, and He imputed their sin to Christ at the cross, and He imputes Christ's righteousness to the elect (2 Corinthians 5:21). Therefore, Christ's righteousness is the only ground and assurance of salvation.

The alone instrument of justification is faith alone (*Sola Fide*). According to heretics, faith precedes regeneration, faith is the cause or ground of salvation, faith plus works save, and faith is not a gift of God. For example, Roman Catholics deny *Sola Fide*, which can be seen in the following excerpt below:

> CANON IX.-If any one saith, that by faith alone the impious is justified; in such wise as to mean, that nothing else is required to co-operate in order to the obtaining the grace of Justification, and that it is not in any way necessary, that he be prepared and disposed by the movement of his own will; **let him be anathema**. (emphasis mine)[65]

But according to the Bible, faith is a gift of God (Ephesians 2:8-9), faith is a work of God, faith is the assurance of things hoped for (Hebrews 11:1),

---

[65] Waterworth, J. (Trans.). (n.d.). *The Council of Trent The Sixth Session: The canons and decrees of the sacred and ecumenical Council of Trent*. Hanover Historical Texts Collection. Retrieved July 19, 2022, from https://history.hanover.edu/texts/trent/ct06.html

faith is the alone instrument whereby God's particular people are united to Christ, and God gives the gift of faith to the elect after they have been born again.

As far as the timing of justification is concerned, the elect of God for whom Christ died were not justified or declared righteous in eternity or at the cross. The Father decreed the justification of the elect in eternity, and the sins of the elect were imputed to Christ at the cross, but the elect are not legally declared righteous until the Holy Spirit irresistibly and efficaciously applies the merits of Christ to the elect in time.

Thus, there is perfect unity and harmony in the operation of the Godhead. The Father chose the elect (Ephesians 1:4), not reprobate, the Son died for the sheep (John 10:11, 15), not goats (John 10:26), and the Spirit seals the invisible church (Ephesians 1:13), not those outside of it. This means the true gospel is grounded in the Father's unconditional election, the Son's particular redemption, and the Spirit's sealing of the invisible church, i.e., the elect of God for whom Christ died.

VI. Closing

This chapter has shown that Roman Catholicism is a denial of the gospel. Paul warned about the dangers of holding to a different gospel in Galatians 1, which states, "But though we, or an angel from heaven, preach any other gospel unto you than that which we have preached unto you, let him be accursed. As we said before, so say I now again, if any man preach any other gospel unto you than that ye have received, let him be accursed" (vv. 8-9).

Therefore, don't ever seek to find neutrality with Roman Catholics because they affirm a false gospel. Witness to Roman Catholics with the true gospel, not with gimmicks, and pray for Roman Catholics. Remember, true love points to truth (*Sola Scriptura*), and true love warns. Thus, the true gospel is the only cure for Roman Catholics. Amen.

STUDY QUESTIONS

1. According to this chapter, Roman Catholicism is a worldview that depends heavily on what?

2. Where do Roman Catholic dogmas derive from?

3. What CCC teaches that a fallible sinner can merit God's grace?

4. Read CCC 2010 and Ephesians 2:8-9, and explain how they differ.

5. Asserting that one can merit God's favor is tantamount to denying what?

6. Do Roman Catholics believe that water baptism is necessary for salvation?

7. What is the doctrine of baptismal regeneration?

8. Is the doctrine of baptismal regeneration heresy?

9. Read CCC 845-846, and explain in your own words why they are not biblical.

10. Is church membership important or necessary for salvation?

11. Do Roman Catholics believe that good works and law-keeping saves?

12. Read CCC 2068, and provide biblical texts that will refute it.

13. How does Genesis 15:6 refute CCC 2068?

14. What is the only cure for Roman Catholics?

15. How is the true gospel grounded in the doctrine of the Trinity?

16. Who is the author of justification?

17. Is the Son eternally subordinate to the Father?

18. What is the source of justification?

19. God's particular grace is reserved exclusively for whom?

20. What is the only ground of justification?

21. What is the whole work of Christ's righteousness in its compact unity?

22. Did Christ die for all men or for the elect?

23. Explain *Sola Fide* in your own words.

24. Explain how there is perfect unity and harmony in the operation of the Godhead.

25. Why is it unbiblical to seek neutrality with Roman Catholics?

Also available on Amazon

(Available in *Kindle & Paperback*)

Also available on Amazon

(Available in *Kindle & Paperback*)

Also available on Amazon

(Available in *Kindle & Paperback*)

About the Author

Sonny Hernandez is pastor of Trinity Gospel Church (KY), and he served 20+ years in the armed forces. He earned a doctorate in pastoral theology/leadership from Tennessee Temple University. He served as an adjunct professor for McKendree University (Radcliff KY Campus) and Grand Canyon University (distance learning). Sonny has authored several books, and has written several published articles for news sources and journals.

TrinityGospelChurchKY.com

ἡ χάρις τοῦ κυρίου Ἰησοῦ
Χριστοῦ καὶ ἡ ἀγάπη τοῦ θεοῦ
καὶ ἡ κοινωνία τοῦ ἁγίου
πνεύματος μετὰ πάντων ὑμῶν